W9-APR-051

MAY 2 0 2013

# Pencils
## BEFORE THE STORE

BY RACHEL LYNETTE • ILLUSTRATED BY DAN McGEEHAN

J674.88
L

Published by The Child's World®
1980 Lookout Drive • Mankato, MN 56003-1705
800-599-READ • www.childsworld.com

ACKNOWLEDGMENTS
The Child's World®: Mary Berendes, Publishing Director
The Design Lab: Design and production
Red Line Editorial: Editorial direction
Content Consultant: S. Jack Hu, Ph.D., J. Reid and Polly Anderson Professor of Manufacturing Technology,
Professor of Mechanical Engineering and Industrial and Operations Engineering, The University of Michigan

Copyright © 2012 by The Child's World®
All rights reserved. No part of this book may be reproduced or utilized in any form or by any means
without written permission from the publisher.

ISBN 9781609736804
LCCN 2011940075

PHOTO CREDITS
Oliver Hoffmann/Dreamstime, cover, 1, back cover; Martin Pietak/Dreamstime, cover (inset), 1 (inset);
Stuart Murray/iStockphoto, 5; Constantine Androsoff/Shutterstock Images, 7, 30; Dmitry Tolkachev/
iStockphoto, 9; Tyler Boyes/Fotolia, 14; Ron Chapple Studios/Dreamstime, 18; Carl Hebert/Bigstock, 19;
Tosporn Preede/iStockphoto, 20; Sondra Paulson/iStockphoto, 21; Kostyantin Pankin/Dreamstime, 22;
Georgii Dolgykh/Dreamstime, 27, 31 (left); Dreamstime, 29, 31 (right)

Design elements: Oliver Hoffmann/Dreamstime

Printed in the United States of America

## ABOUT THE AUTHOR

Rachel Lynette is a big fan of the pencil! She has written more than 100 books for children as well as many teacher resources. She also writes blogs for teachers. Rachel lives near Seattle, Washington. She has a daughter in high school and a son in college.

# Contents

# CHAPTER ONE

# All Kinds of Pencils

People use pencils every day! Little kids who are just learning to write use big, fat pencils. Small, stubby pencils are used at golf courses and libraries. Artists often use colored pencils. Have you used a pencil today?

Have you ever thought about how pencils are made? There are many steps. Take a look at a pencil right now. Look at all the different materials in your pencil. How many do you see? There should be at least three: the part that writes, the wood around it, and the eraser. The first step to making a pencil starts in the forest. That is where the wood comes from!

A single pencil can write more than 45,000 words or draw a line 35 miles (56 km) long!

*Pencils write well on paper.*

# CHAPTER TWO

# In the Forest

Most pencils are made from incense cedar trees. The wood from these trees is perfect for pencils. It does not break easily, but it is soft enough to sharpen. It also does not split or shrink in hot or humid weather. Many people like the smell of cedar wood. Can you imagine the smell of a newly sharpened pencil?

Incense cedar trees grow in central and northern California and the southern part of Oregon. These trees are grown in **sustainable** forests. Foresters are

*Incense cedar trees have wood that is perfect for pencils.*

workers who manage the forests. They plan when trees are cut down and make sure that new trees are planted. That way there will always be new trees growing!

Some kinds of pencils are made from recycled blue jeans.

Incense cedar trees are cut down using chainsaws or large machines. The trees are loaded onto trucks and taken to sawmills. About 300,000 pencils can be made from one large incense cedar tree.

*Trees are cut down to make pencils.*

# CHAPTER THREE

# The Sawmill

At the sawmill, sawing machines are used. These machines cut logs into pencil stock. Pencil stock are long blocks of wood that are all cut to the same size. When they are made into pencils, very little wood is wasted. The pencil stock is dried in a special kiln, or oven. It removes moisture from the wood. Now the pencil stock is ready to be loaded onto trucks or trains to travel to the slat factory.

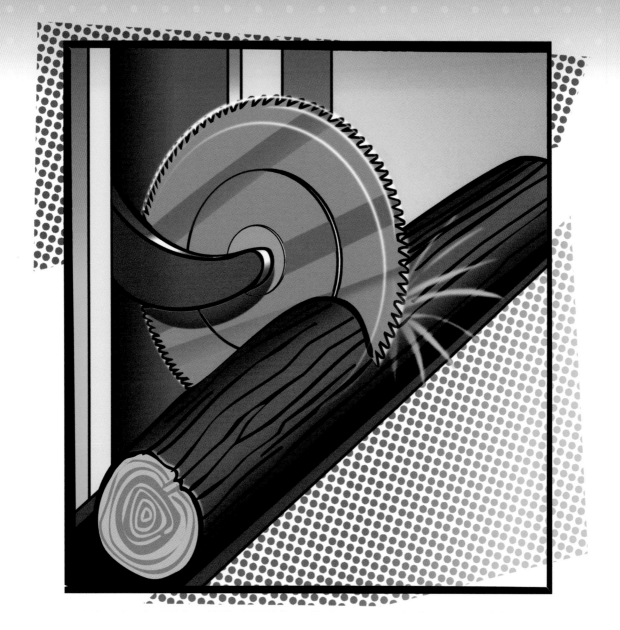

Sawing machines cut the logs.

# CHAPTER FOUR

# The Slat Factory

At the slat factory, the pencil stock is cut into smaller blocks. They are called pencil blocks. The pencil blocks are 8 inches (20 cm) long. Next a circular saw is used. It cuts each block into several very thin pieces, called pencil slats. The slats are treated with stain and wax. This makes the wood all the same color. It also makes the wood easier to work with and sharpen.

Now the slats can be shipped to pencil factories. Often the slats travel by truck or train. If the pencil

factory is on another continent, the slats may be loaded onto ships. Slats that came from trees in California may be shipped all the way to China or Germany to be made into pencils!

*Pencil slats go to the factory to become pencils.*

# CHAPTER FIVE

# At the Pencil Factory

The outside of a pencil is important, but the inside is even more important! The inside is the part that does the writing. It is called the lead, but it is not made from lead. The inside of a pencil is made from a soft **mineral** called **graphite**. At the pencil factory, powdered graphite is mixed with clay and water to make a soft paste. The paste

*The inside of a pencil is made from graphite.*

is pushed through narrow tubes. This forms it into thin, spaghetti-like rods. The rods are cut into pencil-length pieces. Then they are baked in a very hot oven. The heat makes the graphite hard and smooth. Now the leads are ready to be put into pencils.

*Pencil leads are thin and long.*

There is still some work to be done before pencil leads can be put into pencils. When the wood slats get to the factory, they are run under a giant cutting wheel. The wheel cuts six to nine shallow grooves into each slat. The grooves are filled with glue by another machine. Next a third machine places leads in the slats. A second slat is coated with glue and laid on top of the first slat. This is done with a machine called a lead layer. This makes a kind of sandwich with the two grooved slats and the leads in the middle. Finally the slats are put between two clamps. The clamps press the slats together while the glue dries.

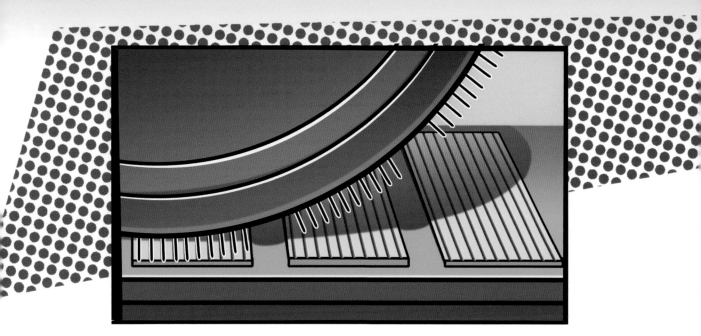

A shaping machine cuts each slat two times. These cuts shape and separate the pencils. The first cut is on the top of the slat. It makes half of the hexagon shape of a pencil. The second cut is made

*Leads are placed in slats by a machine.*

Most pencils are shaped into hexagons. This shape keeps them from rolling off desks.

on the bottom slat. It forms the other half of the hexagon. When that second cut is made, the slat separates into individual pencils. Not all pencils are hexagons. Some pencils have round sides.

*Pencils have a round or hexagon shape.*

Now the pencils are checked for quality. The lead might not be in the center of the pencil. Or the wood may be chipped. A worker sharpens one pencil from each batch by hand. This tests the quality of the lead. Then the tip is tested for strength. The pencil is held in a clamp while a plunger presses on the tip until it breaks. A machine measures how much **pressure** the tip can take before it breaks. If it breaks too soon, the pencil is not sold.

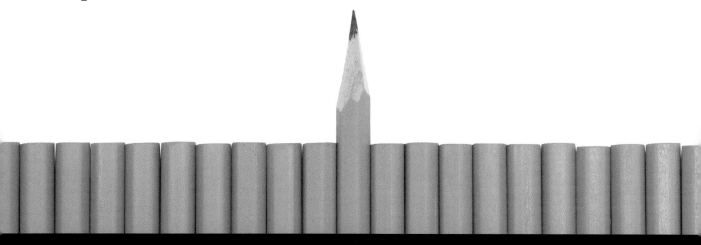

*Workers sharpen one pencil in a batch to test the lead.*

The next step is to paint the pencils. Most pencils in the United States are painted yellow. Sometimes black, red, or even hot pink paints are used. To paint the pencils quickly and evenly, workers run the pencils through a machine. It coats the pencil in paint. A pencil needs at least four coats of paint. Some pencils are coated with paint up to eight times. A final clear coat of **lacquer** is added at the end. It seals the paint and makes the pencil tough and shiny.

*Many are dipped in yellow paint, but pencils can come in all colors.*

Next a machine stamps each pencil. It marks the name of the company that produced it. And it marks a number that tells how hard the lead is. You probably use a number 2 pencil for most of your schoolwork. Artists often use soft leads. You may have also noticed the letters "HB" on your pencil. HB stands for "Hard Black." It tells you that the lead inside the pencil is hard and black.

*The pencils are stamped with the lead number.*

Most pencils have erasers at the top. The eraser may be made at the same factory that makes the pencil. It may also be shipped from a factory that only makes erasers. Pencil erasers are called plugs. Plugs can be made from rubber or **vinyl**. To make the plugs, the raw ingredients are mixed together and heated. In addition to rubber or vinyl, plugs may contain vegetable oil,

*The edges of erasers are rounded.*

**sulfur**, **pumice**, coloring, and other **chemicals**. Then the mixture is forced through a small hole in a machine called an extruder. The mixture comes out of the hole in a long, thin strand. The strands are cut into 3 foot (1 m) pieces. If the strands are made from rubber, they must be heated for the rubber to **cure**. Vinyl does not need to be cured.

Next a machine cuts the strands into tiny plugs. Thousands of plugs are then dumped into a giant drum machine. It spins slowly for several hours. As the plugs tumble against each other, the edges rub together and become rounded.

Now the eraser can be attached to the rest of the pencil. There are several steps. A machine is used to do this job. Can you see the band of metal on a pencil? That metal band is called a **ferrule**. It holds the eraser in place. The pencils move down a **conveyor belt** to the different parts of the machine. Each part has its own job to do.

*Erasers are placed in the ferrules.*

The first part of the machine squeezes or cuts the edges of the top of the pencil. This makes it smaller than the rest of the pencil. Then a plunger slides a ferrule over that end of the pencil. Some pencil factories use glue to keep the ferrule in place. If glue is not used, the ferrule is squeezed onto the pencil. Next the machine places an eraser into the open end of the ferrule. If glue has been used, a plunger pushes the plug into place. If glue has not been used, the machine crimps the ferrule. This keeps the eraser from falling out.

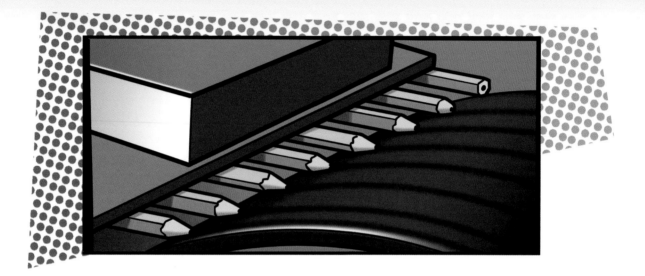

With the eraser in place, the pencil is finished. However, some pencils are sold already sharpened. These pencils are sharpened using a grinding drum. The pencils are rolled across the drum at an angle. This makes the tips touch the drum. When the pencils reach the end of the drum, the pencils have perfect points!

*Pencils are sharpened on a grinding drum.*

Every year more than 14 billion pencils are made in the world. Two billion of those are made in the United States.

Now the pencils are ready to be put into boxes. Machines put just the right number of pencils in each box and seal it. The boxes are put into larger boxes and loaded onto trucks. They are taken to warehouses until it is time for them to be shipped to stores.

*Pencils are boxed and shipped to the store.*

# CHAPTER SIX

# Into Your Hand

You can buy pencils at office supply stores, supermarkets, and variety stores. You may even be able to buy them at your school! Most pencils come in boxes, but sometimes special pencils are sold individually. Have you ever bought a pencil with a purple star eraser? Or do you have one with your school's name on it? These extras do not come from the pencil factory. Another company adds them later.

You need pencils for tests and schoolwork. Or
maybe you like to sketch with them. Having a pencil
is always a good thing. Just remember to bring your
sharpener, too!

*Students use pencils to do schoolwork and take tests.*

# PENCIL MAP

**1**
IN THE FOREST

**2**
AT THE SAWMILL

**6**
ERASERS ADDED

**5**
LEAD PUT IN SLATS

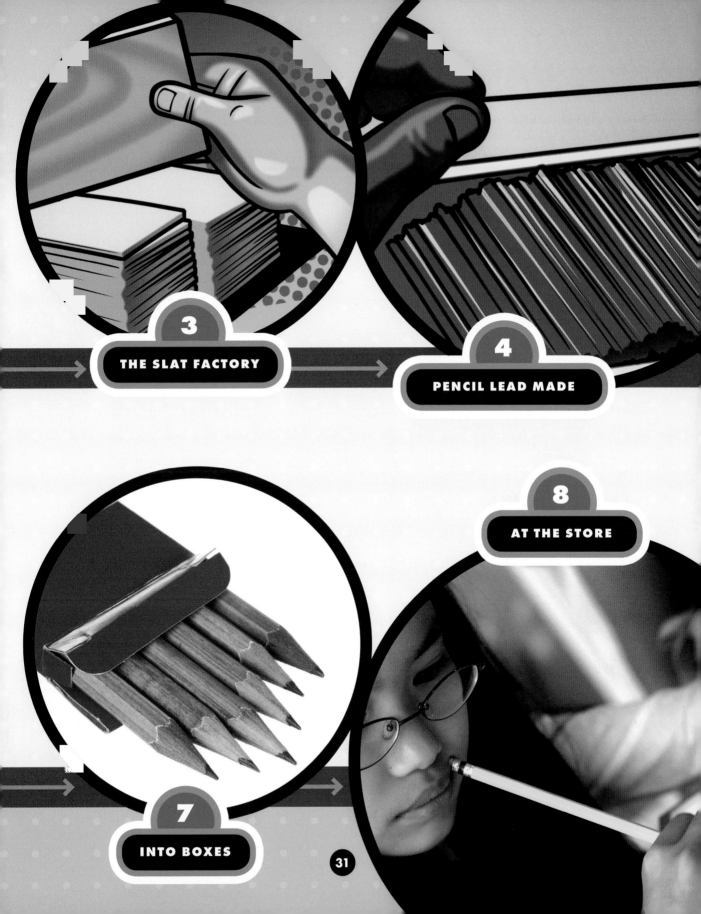

**3**

THE SLAT FACTORY

**4**

PENCIL LEAD MADE

**8**

AT THE STORE

**7**

INTO BOXES

31

## GLOSSARY

**chemicals (KEM-uh-kuhlz):** Chemicals are substances made using chemistry. Different chemicals are used to make erasers.

**conveyor belt (kuhn-VAY-ur BELT):** A conveyor belt is a moving belt that takes materials from one place to another in a factory. Pencils move on a conveyor belt in the factory.

**cure (KYUR):** To cure is to treat something with heat or chemicals to make it last longer. Heat is used to cure rubber erasers.

**ferrule (FER-uhl):** A ferrule is a metal band that is used to connect an eraser to a pencil. A machine pinches the ferrule to the pencil.

**graphite (GRAF-ite):** Graphite is a black or gray mineral that is used as leads in pencils. Graphite is used to make pencil leads.

**lacquer (LAK-ur):** Lacquer is a liquid coating that is put on wood or metal to make it shiny and hard. Lacquer is put over the paint on pencils.

**mineral (MIN-ur-uhl):** A mineral is a material found in nature that is not an animal or plant, such as gold or graphite. Graphite is a mineral used in pencils.

**pressure (PRESH-ur):** Pressure is a force that presses on something. A test measures pressure on the tip of the pencil.

**pumice (PUHM-iss):** Pumice is a light gray rock used in erasers and other products. Pumice helps erasers grind away pencil marks on paper.

**sulfur (SUHL-fur):** Sulfur is a yellow chemical that is used in rubber and other products. Sulfur is in some kinds of erasers.

**sustainable (suh-STAYN-uh-bul):** Something is sustainable if it can be kept going or growing, such as a forest. Foresters make sure the forests are sustainable.

**vinyl (VYE-nuhl):** Vinyl is a light and very strong kind of plastic that is used to make products. Some erasers are made from vinyl.

## BOOKS

Blaxland, Wendy. *Pencils*. New York: Marshall Cavendish Benchmark, 2009.

Cunningham, Kevin. *Pencils*. Ann Arbor, MI: Cherry Lake, 2008.

Hayward, Linda. *I Am a Pencil*. Brookfield, CT: Millbrook Press, 2003.

## INDEX

Visit our Web site for links about pencil production: childsworld.com/links

Note to Parents, Teachers, and Librarians: We routinely verify our Web links to make sure they are safe and active sites. So encourage your readers to check them out!